A Look at Mexico

by Helen Frost

Consulting Editor: Gail Saunders-Smith, Ph.D.

Consultant: Susan Schroeder, Ph.D.
Professor of Colonial Latin American History
Department of History, Tulane University
New Orleans, Louisiana

Pebble Books

an imprint of Capstone Press
Mankato, Minnesota

Pebble Books are published by Capstone Press
151 Good Counsel Drive, P.O. Box 669, Mankato, Minnesota 56002
http://www.capstone-press.com

2 3 4 5 6 07 06 05 04 03 02

Library of Congress Cataloging-in-Publication Data
Frost, Helen, 1949–
    A look at Mexico / by Helen Frost.
    p. cm.—(Our world)
    Includes bibliographical references and index.
    ISBN 0-7368-0985-6 (hardcover)
    ISBN 0-7368-9422-5 (paperback)
    1. Mexico—Juvenile literature. [1. Mexico.] I. Title. II. Series: Our world
(Pebble Books)
F1208.5.F76   2002
972—dc21   00-012784

Summary: Simple text and photographs depict the land, animals, and people
of Mexico.

Note to Parents and Teachers

The series Our World supports national social studies standards
related to culture. This book describes and illustrates the land,
animals, and people of Mexico. The photographs support early
readers in understanding the text. The repetition of words and
phrases helps early readers learn new words. This book also
introduces early readers to subject-specific vocabulary words, which
are defined in the Words to Know section. Early readers may need
assistance to read some words and to use the Table of Contents,
Words to Know, Read More, Internet Sites, and Index/Word List
sections of the book.

Table of Contents

Mexico

Mexico
City ★

Mexico is a country in North America. The capital of Mexico is Mexico City. It is one of the largest cities in the world.

Mexico's flag

desert

rain forest

mountains

6

coast

Mexico has deserts, rain forests, and mountains. Sandy beaches are on Mexico's coasts. Mexico's weather is mostly warm and dry.

toucan

coyote

8

Toucans live in Mexico's rain forests. Coyotes live in Mexico's deserts and mountains.

About 100 million people live in Mexico. Most Mexicans live in cities.

Most Mexicans speak Spanish. Students learn to read and write Spanish in school.

Farmers in Mexico grow coffee, sugarcane, and fruit. Some Mexicans own stores. Mexicans also work in factories to earn money.

Mexico's money is counted in pesos.

Many Mexicans buy their food at outdoor markets. They buy beans, chili peppers, and bananas. Tortillas, tacos, and rice are popular foods in Mexico.

Most Mexicans travel in cars and buses. Some Mexicans ride horses and burros on narrow roads.

People in Mexico built large pyramids long ago. Many people travel to Mexico to see the pyramids.

Words to Know

burro—a small donkey

chili pepper—a small, spicy food used to flavor spicy sauces

desert—a very dry area of land; deserts are sandy or rocky.

pyramid—a structure that is big at the bottom and small at the top; many of the pyramids in Mexico have steps; people climb the steps to reach the top of the pyramid.

rain forest—a tropical forest where a lot of rain falls

sugarcane—a tall, tropical plant; sugarcane has sugar in its woody stems.

taco—a Mexican food made up of a fried tortilla folded around meat or cheese

tortilla—a round, flat bread that is made from cornmeal or flour

Read More

Alcraft, Rob. *Mexico.* A Visit to. Des Plaines, Ill.: Heinemann Library, 1999.

Berendes, Mary. *Mexico.* Faces and Places. Plymouth, Minn.: Child's World, 1998.

Dahl, Michael. *Mexico.* Countries of the World. Mankato, Minn.: Bridgestone Books, 1997.

Jermyn, Leslie, and Fiona Conboy. *Welcome to Mexico.* Welcome to My Country. Milwaukee: Gareth Stevens, 1999.

Internet Sites

All You Ever Wanted to Know about Mexico!
http://tqjunior.thinkquest.org/6089

Mexico for Kids
http://www.elbalero.gob.mx/kids

Zoom School: Mexico
http://www.zoomschool.com/school/Mexico

Index/Word List

beaches, 7
burros, 19
buses, 19
cars, 19
cities, 5, 11
country, 5
coyotes, 9
deserts, 7, 9
fruit, 15

horses, 19
live, 9, 11
markets, 17
Mexicans, 11,
   13, 15, 17, 19
Mexico City, 5
money, 15
mountains, 7, 9
North America, 5

people, 11
pyramids, 21
rain forests, 7, 9
roads, 19
school, 13
Spanish, 13
students, 13
toucans, 9
travel, 19, 21

Word Count: 159
Early-Intervention Level: 16

Editorial Credits

Mari C. Schuh, editor; Kia Bielke, cover designer and illustrator; Kimberly Danger, photo researcher

Photo Credits

Corel/Richard Jackson, 8 (right)
Digital Stock, 1, 6 (lower right), 10
International Stock/Cliff Hollenbeck, cover, 14
Mary and Lloyd McCarthy/Root Resources, 8 (left)
Michele Burgess, 6 (upper left)
Photo Network/Grace Davies, 20
Rob and Ann Simpson, 6 (upper right)
Robert & Linda Mitchell, 16, 18
Unicorn Stock Photos/Kathi Corder, 18 (inset)
Visuals Unlimited, 6 (lower left); Visuals Unlimited/Jeff Greenberg, 12

The author thanks the children's section staff at the Allen County Public Library in Fort Wayne, Indiana, for research assistance.

24